J
591.5   Hess, Lilo   C. 3
             Secrets in the
          meadow

DATE DUE

J
591.5   Hess, Lilo   C. 3
             Secrets in the
          meadow
                                    13.95

DATE		ISSUED TO
SEP 17 1987	4	DISCARDED
OCT 15 1987	6	
MAY 0 8 1989	1	

READING IS COOL

This book has been donated
by the Friends of the Library
in recognition of the achievement of

Larch Laws

during the "Reading is Cool"
Summer Reading Program, 1987.
Lake County Library

Secrets in the Meadow

Secrets in the Meadow

Lilo Hess

Charles Scribner's Sons · New York

Library of Congress Cataloging-in-Publication Data
Hess, Lilo.   Secrets in the meadow.
Includes index.
Summary: Describes the many animals to be found in a meadow,
seemingly a serene place, yet teeming with life in the form of deer,
rabbits, ants, spiders, raccoons, bats, and other creatures.
1. Meadow ecology—Juvenile literature. [1. Meadow animals] I. Title.
QH541.5.M4H47 1986   591.5′2643   85-43350
ISBN 0-684-18525-3

1 3 5 7 9 11 13 15 17 19 HAL 20 18 16 14 12 10 8 6 4 2

Printed in the United States of America

A meadow contains many different grasses, wild flowers, weeds, a few bushes, and sometimes a tree. It is often bordered by a small stream, a river, or a pond on one side, and woodland on the other. A meadow always looks peaceful and serene. But is it really so?

Most of the many creatures that live in a meadow are seldom seen. Their lives are secretive, quiet, and short. A meadow is a world in miniature. Its inhabitants are builders, weavers, herdsmen, hunters, and assassins. There are also soldiers, actors, and musicians. Love, birth, and death can be found in a meadow, but only if one is patient and observes closely.

5

Larger animals also use the meadow. They feed there, find temporary shelter in it, or romp in its tall weeds. We need not know the scientific name of each species of animal to feel and observe how beautifully it fits into the meadow and gives it its unique character.

If we look closely into this clump of weeds, we can see a pair of soft, dark eyes following every move we make. They belong to a fawn, only ten or twelve hours old. It was born the evening before in the adjoining woodlot. The birth had gone smoothly. The experienced doe had licked the baby over and over to clean and dry it and to stimulate its circulation. Then she nudged it to stand. The baby tried several times, only to have its matchstick-like legs buckle under it. Finally, on the fourth try, the little fawn stood and immediately started to suckle. When it had fin-

ished, the doe made her fawn walk a few steps; then both of them bedded down for the night.

Very early in the morning the fawn follows its mother with stiff hops and jumps into the meadow. There the fawn lies down in the tall weeds while the doe goes off to graze as she does every day.

The fawn is well hidden from enemies, and it has no telltale body odor for the first few weeks of its life, which also protects it from predators. The doe rests in the grass after she has finished eating, but she lies off to the side of the fawn, instead of close by. Should an enemy go too close to her baby, she will divert its attention by running away from the fawn's hiding place, trying to make it pursue her and forget about the fawn.

People often think that a baby animal is abandoned when they see one alone. That is hardly ever so, and the baby is best left where it is. Only if one knows for sure that the mother is dead, should a wild baby be rescued.

Just about fifteen feet from where the fawn is hiding, a female rabbit, also called a doe, sits motionless. Her brown and gray mottled fur blends well with the green and brown grasses and the soil. She is keeping an eye on a well-concealed blanket of

grass, leaves, and twigs. Under the blanket, in a shallow depression of the soil, sleep three baby rabbits. No movement or noise reveals their presence. The doe will also run away from the nest site should an enemy get too close. She might even pretend to stumble or limp as if injured to make it follow her and leave her babies unharmed. A turtle, looking for berries, walks right over the nest, but the doe does not get alarmed; she knows that the turtle is no threat. When all is quiet, the doe hops over to the nest, pushes the cover away, and checks her babies. As soon as the young feel their mother nuzzling them, they squeal and start to nurse.

10

Baby rabbits grow quickly. When they are about sixteen days old, they leave the nest. For a short time they stay together, sleeping under bushes or in a clump of grass. They play tag and hide-and-seek, and they discover new and good things to eat. After about a week they separate, each going its own way. Soon they will find mates and raise their own families.

Ants are always busy in the meadow. It seems that they never rest or sleep. There are many kinds of ants, and they make their homes in different places. Some live under stones, some live in holes in the ground, while others build above-ground mounds. Ants can be red, orange, gray, or black. Some are tiny, others quite large. All have very organized and regulated lives. Only the queen lays eggs. In contrast to bees or wasps, who have only one queen per colony, ants can have several. Workers take care of every chore in the nest except its defense. That is the job of the soldier ants. Workers who provide the food for the colony sometimes kill other insects or drag home the bodies of dead ones. When a dead insect is too large for one ant to move, it will summon other workers to help, but not before it has struggled alone for some time.

Another early riser in the meadow is the spider. Nothing looks prettier than a spider's delicate web, with glistening dewdrops clinging to it. But not all webs are intact in the early morning hours. Many get torn or destroyed when night animals walk through them. Sometimes a large insect gets entangled in a web and tears it in trying to free itself. A spider must constantly repair its snare by releasing silk stored in glands of the *abdomen*.* These glands are called *spinnerets*.

*Words in italics are defined in the glossary, page 63.

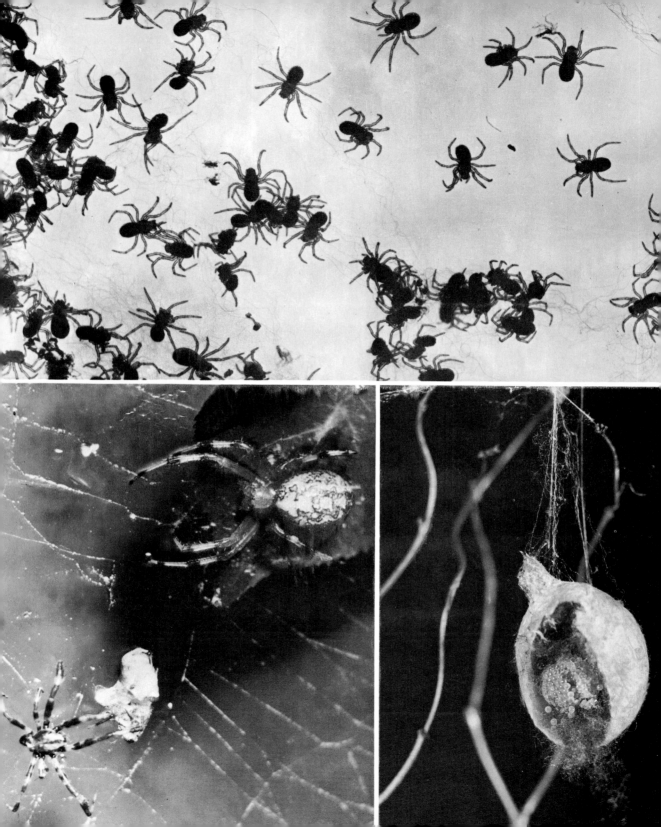

Different spiders construct different webs, and some make no web at all. Spiders are not insects; they belong to a class called Arachnida. True insects have six legs, but the arachnida have eight. They have no *antennae*, their eyes are small and simple, and the head and *thorax* are fused together. Scorpions and centipedes, among others, belong to this group.

A total of forty thousand spider species live all over the world. People are often afraid of spiders, but most are completely harmless to man. Although spiders can bite, even the bite of the feared black widow is not usually fatal. The deaths that occur in connection with such a bite usually are caused by other medical complications. But a bite from a poisonous spider should not be taken lightly and should be treated similarly to that of a poisonous snake.

When the female spider is ready to mate, a male approaches her very cautiously. He runs great risk of being eaten by his bride, which is much larger than he. As soon as the mating is over he beats a hasty retreat. Several days later the female deposits her eggs in a well-insulated silken pouch that she had spun and secured to sturdy weed stalks. Different spiders have different ways of constructing egg sacks and of caring for the eggs or the young. When the little meadow spiders hatch, they look like miniature adults. If the weather is cold, they remain inside the egg sack until spring. Some spiders live just one year; others, such as the tarantulas, are supposed to live twenty-five to thirty years.

Early morning in the meadow is often a time for birth. For the promethea moth it is a new cycle. All winter long a small brown *cocoon* has weathered winds and snowstorms securely attached to a wild grape vine at the edge of the meadow. It was put there last fall by a green caterpillar with red spots and silvery lines. The caterpillar had first spun silken threads around the twig and fastened a leaf to it. Then it had wrapped the leaf around itself like a sheath and fastened the edges together. Inside the leaf it had woven a cocoon, leaving a small opening on the top. Within the cocoon the miraculous rearrangement of tissues called *metamorphosis* had taken place. It had transformed the caterpillar into the adult form of the insect. When the great change was completed, usually in the late spring or

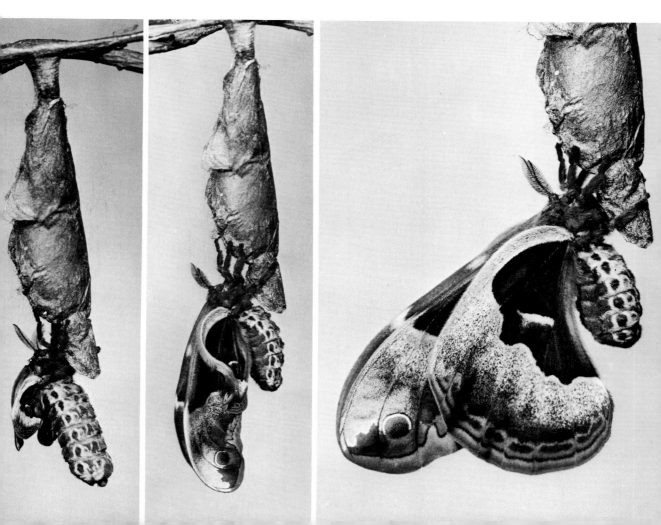

summer, the new creature emerged. It looked withered, crumpled, and drooping. It stretched and quivered and then pumped fluids into the veins of its wings. Slowly the wings unfolded. After about twenty minutes they were smooth and stiff. After excess liquid was discharged from its body, the handsome moth was ready to fly. A few days after emerging, the promethea moth looks for a mate. After mating, the moths die, but not before the female lays her eggs. The eggs hatch in about forty-eight days, tiny caterpillars emerge, and when they are fully grown the cycle repeats itself.

In the middle of the meadow, an almost identical process is taking place. The familiar black and orange monarch butterfly, which has just emerged, is pumping fluids into its limp wings. The difference between a butterfly and a moth can be seen in their antennae. The butterfly has a knob at the end of its antenna; the moth's is either feathery or smooth-pointed. Moths, with just a few exceptions, fly at night, but all butterflies are day fliers.

18

The *larva* of the monarch is a boldly striped caterpillar whose colors are black, white, and creamy yellow. It eats only milkweed plants. It sheds its skin several times as it matures. When it is fully grown it suspends itself on the underside of a leaf or a twig and sheds its skin for the last time, revealing the *pupa* or *chrysalis*, a jade green nugget studded with golden dots. Inside, the reorganization of the caterpillar into the butterfly takes about a week. Just before the butterfly emerges, the chrysalis

becomes transparent, revealing the delicate insect inside. Then it splits open and the monarch butterfly struggles out.

Unlike the promethea moth, the monarch usually does not die when winter sets in. Because it lives longer, it has to eat, while the moth does not. The monarch sips nectar from flowers through a long tube, which curls up when not in use.

In the fall, before it gets too cold, most of the monarchs migrate to a warmer climate. They fly to Mexico, Florida, or Southern California, depending from where they start. They are guided by a sense that is still not fully understood. Some monarchs die on the way, some mate and die in their winter home, but in the spring, the new and the surviving monarchs fly back north, to mate and lay their eggs on milkweed plants in meadows and along the roadsides.

Another creature that can be observed early in the morning as well as in the evening, when the atmosphere is moist and cool in the meadow, is the earthworm.

Although this worm lives underground in burrows, it surfaces from time to time and crawls about. It never ventures far from its tunnels, and returns as soon as the sun rises. Earthworms can plow through almost any kind of soil in search of food, which consists of organic matter such as roots, decaying leaves, and

other vegetation. Their tunnels *aerate* the soil by letting rain and air circulate through it. Earthworm droppings, called castings, make rich fertilizer that is collected and sold commercially. Earthworms mate, lay eggs, are born, and die underground.

All over the meadow we can see little foamy masses clinging to weeds and grasses. Those are the bubble houses of a tiny insect called the froghopper or spittlebug. This insect sucks the juices out of the stems of the weeds on which it lives with a sharp little beak. When the wingless baby froghopper starts its house, it forces out liquid and air from a chamber in its abdomen. The effect is much like blowing bubbles. When it has completely covered itself with this foam, it stops. The frothy mass probably protects the young hopper from the hot sun and from enemies. When the froghopper grows, it sheds its skin several times. After the last *molt*, the mature insect emerges. It is green and tan, has wings, and is about one-tenth of an inch long. Now it leaves its bubble nest and flies about in the meadow. In the fall it mates, the female lays her eggs, and both male and female die. The eggs hatch the following spring and new bubble nests appear.

23

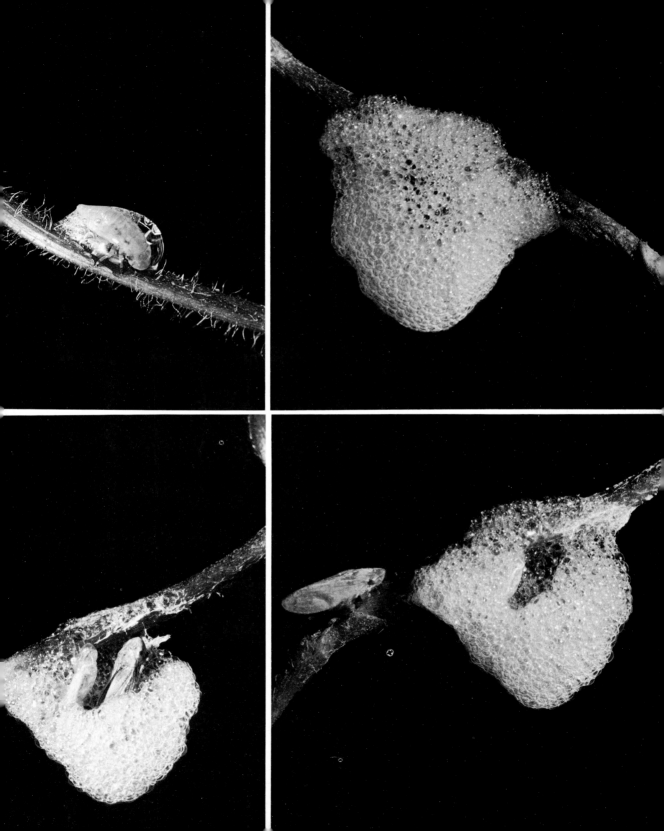

There are other little insects, of various shapes and sizes, that suck juices out of plants. Some are called leafhoppers, others are treehoppers or insect brownies.

In the lower end of the meadow is a dead tree. The bark has rotted away, and moss and lichen grow on one side. A tubular structure of mud clings to a crevice on the other side of the tree. It is about three inches long. A slender wasp adds more dabs of mud to this strange nest. It is the mud dauber. Male and female mud dauber wasps, who are skilled masons, are working closely together. When one wasp flies off to collect more soft mud from rain puddles or the nearby stream, the other comes and adds its supply of mud to the structure. When the nest is finished, the wasps collect little spiders or other small insects, which they

paralyze and stuff into the chambers of their nest. As soon as the chambers are filled with victims, the female wasp lays her eggs on them. This way the young larvae have fresh, live food to eat when they hatch. Different species of mud daubers make different-shaped nests, but all provide live food for their young.

Another little creature lives in the rotted wood of the dead tree. It is a beetle called the click beetle or skipjack, of the family Elateridae. This insect acrobat performs an amazing stunt. When threatened or frightened, it drops to the ground, usually falling on its back, playing dead. When all danger has passed, it propels itself, with an audible click, into the air to right itself. Then it scurries away. Sometimes it has to snap its thorax twice in order to land on its feet.

There are several species of click beetle. Some are very tiny;
others, like the eyed elater here, can be from a half-inch to
almost two inches long. The eye-like markings are just a bluff.
The real, very small eyes are located on either side of the head.
The beetle eats decaying wood.

Right behind the dead tree is a patch of brambles, and in it
another kind of wasp is constructing its nest. It is the fierce
white-faced paper wasp. An entire colony of wasps constructs
this large globular nest, which is often seen against country
houses and barns, or in trees, bushes, and even abandoned cars.

A new nest is started every year by a fertilized queen, who alone has survived the winter. In the spring she lays eggs that produce her future helpers. As soon as the workers, all females, have hatched, they take over the job of constructing the nest. They also provide food and care for their queen, themselves, and the new eggs and larvae. The queen becomes an egg-laying machine. To make the paper-like material for the nest, the wasps chew pieces of old rotted wood and mix it with their saliva. They painstakingly add a mouthful at a time to the nest to make it larger and larger. They gather nectar and pollen to feed the larvae, which is the future generation of workers. The wasps keep the larvae very clean and help the new wasps to hatch, when their time comes.

Feeding larvae

Adding paper

At one time in the life of the queen, she lays special eggs that hatch into either males or other queens. The males later fertilize the new queens, and they die when it gets cold. So do all the working wasps. The queens hibernate in sheltered places during the winter months and emerge the following spring to start new colonies.

By mid-morning more and more creatures can be seen in the meadow. We call most insects "bugs," but not all are true bugs. Bugs have thin, clear wings under a colored leathery outer covering. They all have a mouth shaped like a tube, ending in a sharp point called a *proboscis*. With this they suck out juices from plants or animals. In the meadow there is a half-inch fierce assassin called the ambush bug. It lurks hidden in flowers until an insect approaches. Then it strikes swiftly with tiny clawed front feet. It seldom misses. It catches bumblebees, hornets, and other insects much larger than itself. After sucking its victims dry, the ambush bug flings away the remains and waits for its next meal.

Scurrying through the tall weeds is the green stink bug, who is always looking for a meal. When it catches a victim, such as a plump, juicy grub, the stink bug drags it to a comfortable, undisturbed place to consume it. This bug belongs to a large group consisting of many hundred species that are divided by their preference in food. Some are vegetarians, sucking the sap of plants; others feed on insects. All stink bugs have scent glands on the underside of their thorax that have openings in the base of the hindlegs. When frightened they can release the scent and spray their surroundings with an evil-smelling and vile-tasting substance. Some stink bugs are brightly colored, but most of the meadow residents are green or brown.

By mid-afternoon the meadow shimmers in the hot sun and is very quiet. Many insects crawl under leaves, between blades of grass, or under stones to keep cool. Birds and mammals seek out the shade of bushes or nearby trees. But one large fly buzzes loudly while it flies over the meadow no matter how hot it is. This is the robber fly. When it spots a meal, it pounces on it in flight, holding the victim with long spindly legs. Then it settles on a leaf, a flower, or a twig to devour it leisurely by sucking out its juices. After the meal it cleans itself and is off to hunt again. Its diet includes everything from bumblebees to mosquitoes. The vision of the robber fly is very keen. The enormous eyes have over four thousand separate little lenses.

A slender insect sits on a twig in the meadow swaying back and forth as if moved by a gentle wind. This is the praying mantis. It is called an assassin, because the way it catches its food and eats it alive seems cruel to us.

The mantis can move its head from side to side and up and down, so it can spot and follow its victim anywhere. Its eyes are large and its vision is keen. When the intended victim is within striking distance, the mantis shoots out its toothed forelegs like lightning, grabs the prey tightly, and then consumes it leisurely.

The half-grown mantis we see this early summer afternoon hatched from an egg just about a month ago. All its many sisters and brothers hatched at the same time. They wriggled and tumbled out of the egg mass and scattered as quickly as they could. If they had lingered, the stronger ones would have eaten the weaker and smaller ones. All the baby mantises were vulnerable because their bodies were still soft. Birds, spiders, frogs, newts, and larger insects consider them a delicate morsel.

The surviving mantises ate tiny insects at first and larger ones as they became stronger and bigger. In the fall they will be fully grown and have wings. At mating time a male approaches a female very carefully and beats a hasty retreat right afterward. If the female catches him, she will devour him.

Several days after mating, the female lays her eggs on sturdy weeds and twigs. Through glands in her body she whips up a cream-colored froth, and in it deposits forty to four hundred eggs. After a few hours the frothy mass hardens, enabling it to survive rain, wind, and snowstorms. Both the male and the female mantises die when the weather turns cold.

No meadow is complete without the little red beetles with the black spots. Ladybeetles (misnamed ladybugs) crawl busily up and down grasses, weeds, and flower stems in search of *aphids*, red spiders, tiny larvae, and even small beetle eggs, which they consume in large quantities. They are great helpers to farmers and gardeners, who often buy them by the pound and release them in their fields, gardens, and orchards. The beetles are collected high in the Sierra Mountains and other mountainous places where they hibernate in great numbers, after they have migrated there from their summer homes. But not all ladybeetles migrate. Some spend the winter in cracks of houses or under stones, loose bark, or windowsills close to their homes in meadow, field, or garden. When spring comes they awaken and hungrily go to work consuming insect pests. Different species have different markings, and some vary in body color, which may be yellow, orange, or black.

Many rhymes in many languages have been sung or recited about ladybeetles by children. One popular song is:

> Ladybird, ladybird,
> Fly away home.
> Your house is on fire and
> Your children will burn.

The name "ladybird" was probably given to these little insects in the Middle Ages when it was believed that they watched over the Virgin Mary. The other lines might have originated in a country where hop vines, from which beer is made, were raised. Ladybeetles ate the aphids that infected the hop plants. After the harvest the hop fields were burned over, and the

40

beetles had to fly away if they were to save themselves. They could not have saved their children, though, since they have no way of knowing them.

Ladybeetles in the meadow lay eggs on the underside of leaves or weeds. When they hatch, the prickly looking larvae start to eat immediately. The larva eats the same food that the adult insect likes, and it grows rapidly. When it is fully grown, about a quarter- to a half-inch long, it fastens itself by its tail to a leaf or another plant in the meadow and changes into a pupa. About a week later the skin splits open and the adult emerges. Some of the red ladybeetles are pale cream or yellow when they first hatch. It may take an hour or more for the wing case to harden and turn red with the familiar black spots.

Grasshoppers live in meadows, gardens, and along roadsides. They are small and do no real harm to the vegetation they eat. The males of the many species are the musicians. They make their sound by rasping their wings together. Unlike the cicadas and the katydids, grasshoppers make their music during the daytime. They are very muscular and can make remarkably long leaps for a quick getaway when we disturb them while walking through the meadow grass. Baby grasshoppers are similar to the adults, except that they are small and have no wings.

A close relative of our grasshopper is the locust. These insects can damage crops very badly. They sometimes multiply in such numbers that they darken the sky as they eat their way through one field after another, even stripping leaves off the trees.

Once in a while in the late afternoon a black bear and her cub visit the meadow. While the bouncy cub frolics in the tall grass, its mother is searching for berries, new buds, and other morsels nearby. When she finds an underground bees' or wasps' nest, she digs it up to eat the grubs, honey, and pollen. She seems unconcerned about the angry insects that swarm about her.

The bear cub nibbles on berries, buds, or flowers, but mother's milk is still its main food. The cub was born in a den in the cold of winter. It was very tiny, blind, and helpless at first, but it grew fast. Since the beginning of spring it has followed its mother everywhere she goes. When the cub gets tired of playing, it lies down and takes a nap in the grass. It is very exciting to come upon a cute, cuddly bear cub in the meadow, but beware—its mother is never far away and is very protective.

45

Unless we are very quiet and look closely, we will probably never see the many mice scurrying through the meadow during the day as well as during the night hours. Three species can be found here: the deer mouse, the white-footed mouse, and the meadow vole. The deer mouse and the white-footed mouse look so much alike that only an expert can tell them apart. They are of a rich brown or grayish color and have white feet and a white chest. The voles, which are more numerous than the other two species, are of a drab brown color. Probably no creature is hunted and devoured by other creatures as much as mice. But they breed so frequently that their numbers remain stable.

Right here in the meadow are many mouse nests. They are in a clump of grass, in tall weeds, under bushes or rocks, and sometimes, like this white-footed mouse's, in an empty bird's nest. Anywhere there is a little shelter and safety, a mouse will make its nest. A nest can be made of grass, moss, or little twigs. It is usually lined with something soft such as chewed-up paper, fluffy seeds, or feathers. Two to six naked and helpless young are born several times a year. The female mouse feeds, cleans, and protects them. If the mother feels that the nest has been discovered, she picks the babies up in her mouth and moves them one by one to a safer place. The young grow quickly, and at the age of two months they are on their own and ready to start a new family.

48

All through the day the residents of the meadow are occupied with fighting for survival, hunting, playing, home-building, and other domestic activities, but when the sun sets and the sky darkens, almost all the day-loving creatures go to sleep or hide. Now is the time for *nocturnal* animals to emerge from their hiding places.

Anyone who has ever spent a summer evening in the country, especially near a meadow, has heard the night music of the cicadas. This shrill sound is made only by the male, who has two drum-like chambers, one on each side of the abdomen. When the chambers are vibrated, the "song" is heard loud and clear.

Cicadas are often mistakenly called "locusts," but the true locust belongs to the grasshopper family. There are about 1,500 species of cicadas in the world. The best known is probably what is misnamed the "seventeen-year locust." The female lays her eggs into twigs by means of a sharp-pointed *ovipositor*. When the *nymph* hatches, it falls to the ground and immediately burrows underground. The nymph feeds on roots and moves about with the help of strong shovel-like front feet. After seventeen years it is fully grown and emerges from the ground. It climbs

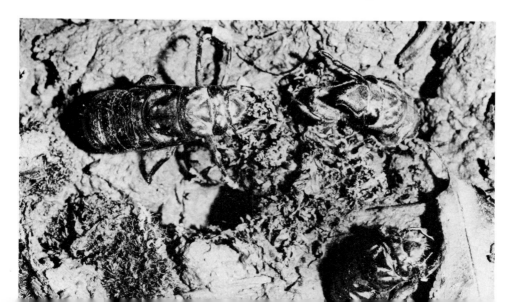

up the nearest object—a weed, a twig, a tree trunk, or the wall of a building. After a few minutes' rest it splits its skin and steps out as a winged adult. The empty, ghost-like skin is left behind.

Another nightly serenader is the katydid. Different species make various sounds. The male katydid of the familiar green species sits on a weed in the meadow and rasps its wings together three times, making the famous song that sounds like "katy-did." When he rubs them together twice, it sounds like "she didn't." Some scientists have estimated that this insect rubs its wings together fifty million times during one season. The female katydid, for whose benefit this music is produced, hears it with ears located on her front legs near the elbow. She cannot sing herself, but she follows the sound to meet her mate. Katydids are hard to find, because they blend in so well with their surroundings.

As night settles over the meadow, small and large moths, and nocturnal beetles, bugs, birds, and mammals awaken. Some animals, such as mice and mosquitoes, are active at night as well as during the day. Others can best be observed when it is dark.

The little dots of light twinkling in the summer meadow are the fireflies. They are soft-bodied beetles. During the day it is hard to see them, but they are easy to spot in the pale moonlight crawling up and down grasses and weeds, even if they are not flashing their little light beams. The light of fireflies is called "cold light," because it produces very little heat. The fireflies use these flashes to communicate with one another. Scientists think that it is not so much the flashing light but the intervals between the flashes that are the code of communication. More than two thousand species of fireflies are known; fifty species inhabit the United States.

At the lower end of the meadow a fox steps out of the woods cautiously. He knows the meadow well. He and his mate, the vixen, have hunted here for several years. Other foxes also come to the meadow for their food, but they stay out of each others' way. Besides hunting for mice and an occasional rabbit, the foxes eat the fruit and berries in season. If nothing else is available, they content themselves with insects, grubs, or dead animals. The fox and his mate communicate with each other by barks. When they have young ones in the den, they must catch enough food for the entire family. As soon as the baby foxes are old enough they follow their parents to the meadow to learn to hunt and play.

The opossum also feeds in the meadow. It has few enemies because it is a formidable fighter and is quick to use its many sharp teeth to defend itself. When everything else fails, it uses its famous bluff and plays dead. At night in the meadow it searches for berries, grubs, insects, and small mammals if it can catch them. It will also eat the eggs of low-nesting birds. Young opossums often cling to their mothers' backs to go along on the nightly foraging trips. This way they learn what an opossum eats and how to catch it.

Raccoons usually visit the meadow at night, but sometimes they get bold and come out of hiding during the daytime. They are very fond of various berries, nuts, seeds, and fruits, but they also eat some eggs, meat, insects, grubs, and snails. In the fall, when the apples and grapes are ripe, raccoons will seek them out and gorge themselves until the supply dries up.

56

High above the meadow, darting so rapidly that one can hardly make out its shape, flies a bat. Round and round it goes in ever-widening circles. It is hunting small flying insects such as mosquitoes, and every night it consumes its own weight in prey. It seems to us that it glides silently through the air, but in reality the bat emits constant sounds, so high-pitched that the human ear cannot detect them. When this high note meets an object, such as a small flying insect, an echo bounces off the insect back to the bat's ear. This way the bat can tell where and how far away its quarry is. Although bats are very beneficial to man and quite harmless, they are relentlessly persecuted. Sensationalized and exaggerated reports about bats that are rabid, entangle themselves in people's hair, drink human blood, kill livestock, destroy crops, or bite children keep fear alive.

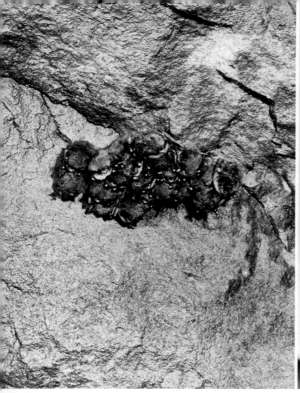 

Different kinds of bats are found all over the world. They are mammals that reproduce slowly and shun the sunlight. They live in caves, rock outcroppings, trees, barns, attics, and other secluded places. Although their vision is poor, they are not blind. Bats usually live in groups, and most are insect eaters. Some species sip the nectar of flowers, and the infamous vampire bat drinks blood from a small bite it makes on cattle, much as the mosquito sucks human blood.

Bats can get rabies just like other wild mammals, but this happens much less often than many reports would have us believe. Yet one should never pick up a wild bat by hand, and one should stay away from a bat that flutters about close to the ground in daylight or that seems almost tame. A healthy bat will not attack, but will bite when frightened.

Where the meadow ends and the woods begin, three baby owls sit on a limb and wait for their parents to bring back the mice they catch in the meadow.

Many other creatures are active at night. Night-flying moths like the cecropia moth find their mates in the dark, attracted to them by scent. Newts, salamanders, snails, and toads venture out from cool, damp hiding places in search of food; they shun the daytime with its warmer atmosphere, because their skin dries out easily.

As soon as the darkness starts to lift, most of those night creatures retire and go to sleep. But the meadow does not stay empty and quiet for long. Before the first rays of daylight are visible, birds start to sing, rabbits are hopping about, and ants and spiders start their busy day's work. Another day is starting in the meadow, just like other early summer days have started for years. By mid-morning, though, something has changed. Several men, carrying surveying instruments, walk across the meadow.

60

Ladybeetle just manages to fly off before being crushed by heavy boots. Some little caterpillars and ants are not so lucky. The spider's web gets torn, but the baby rabbits remain unhurt in their shallow nest, even though the men walk right over it.

At one end of the meadow the men cut a narrow strip of grass and weeds and set up their equipment. One of the men goes to the far side, signaling to the other, who measures, with an instrument called a transit, the boundary lines to calculate the size of the property. All the inhabitants of the meadow fall silent until the men leave several hours later. Then life in the meadow continues as always.

But for how long? A development of houses has been planned for this site. Where will all the animals go? Will there be enough meadow left for all the small and large creatures to pursue their short and secret lives?

GLOSSARY

ABDOMEN: in insects, the rear section of the body

AERATE: to combine with air

ANTENNA (plural, *antennae*): jointed feelers on the heads of many insects that serve as organs of touch; some antennae contain other sense organs as well, such as those for smelling, hearing, tasting, and detecting temperature changes

APHID: a small insect that feeds on plants by sucking their juices

CHRYSALIS: the stage through which some insects pass before they become adults, during which they undergo changes in structure; also, the protective outer covering in which the larva remains during the chrysalis stage

COCOON: a protective case inside of which the body of some insects undergoes changes before the adult stage

LARVA (plural, *larvae*): an immature insect

METAMORPHOSIS: a process that changes an immature insect into its adult form. Some insects go through complete metamorphosis, when the newly hatched young do not resemble the adult; their life cycle consists of four stages—egg, larva, pupa (or chrysalis), adult. Other insects go through incomplete metamorphosis, when the newly hatched young resembles the adult but is not exactly the same.

MOLT: to shed the skin or outer body covering

NOCTURNAL: active at night

NYMPH: an insect in the larval stage that goes through incomplete metamorphosis

OVIPOSITOR: a specialized organ in certain insects for depositing eggs

PROBOSCIS: a long, tube-like snout

PUPA: a chrysalis, or the chrysalis stage in the life of an insect

SPINNERETS: the organ in spiders that secretes the silk they use to spin a web

THORAX: in insects, the middle section of the body

INDEX